GIVE THIS BOOK A COVER

SPARK YOUR IMAGINATION with OVER 100 ACTIVITIES

BY JARRETT LERNER AND YOU!

ALADDIN
New York London Toronto Sydney New Delhi

For the creator
within YOU

ALADDIN
An imprint of Simon & Schuster Children's Publishing Division
1230 Avenue of the Americas, New York, New York 10020
First Aladdin edition May 2021
Copyright © 2021 by Jarrett Lerner
All rights reserved, including the right of reproduction
in whole or in part in any form.
ALADDIN and related logo are registered trademarks
of Simon & Schuster, Inc.
For information about special discounts for bulk purchases, please contact
Simon & Schuster Special Sales at 1-866-506-1949
or business@simonandschuster.com.
The Simon & Schuster Speakers Bureau can bring authors to your live event.
For more information or to book an event contact the Simon & Schuster
Speakers Bureau at 1-866-248-3049 or visit our website
at www.simonspeakers.com.
Designed by Alicia Mikles
The illustrations for this book were rendered in Procreate.
The text of this book was set in Give This Font a Name.
Manufactured in the United States of America 0321 NGS
2 4 6 8 10 9 7 5 3 1
ISBN 978-1-5344-8981-3

If you're holding this book, it's probably because you're curious about creativity. Especially YOUR creativity.

The most important thing you need to know about creativity is this:

THERE IS NO RIGHT OR WRONG WAY TO CREATE.

In this book, you'll learn a lot about how I create. You'll learn, for instance, how I draw bats and hats and even helicopters. You'll see the sorts of questions I ask myself to find ideas for stories. I'm sharing it all not because these are the correct or only ways of doing all this, but in the hopes that it helps you further explore your own creativity and discover your own unique ways of creating.

There's also no right or wrong way to use this book. You can start at the beginning and work your way to the end. Or you can start at the back and work your way to the front. You can even just jump around and do activities at random! However you use this book, I hope it provides a little bit of instruction and A LOT of inspiration. I hope it serves as a launchpad, helping you reach new creative heights.

One last thing, and maybe the most important thing:
don't forget to HAVE FUN.

JARRett!!

Who do you like spending time with?
Can you draw a picture of them?

HOW to DRAW a FISH

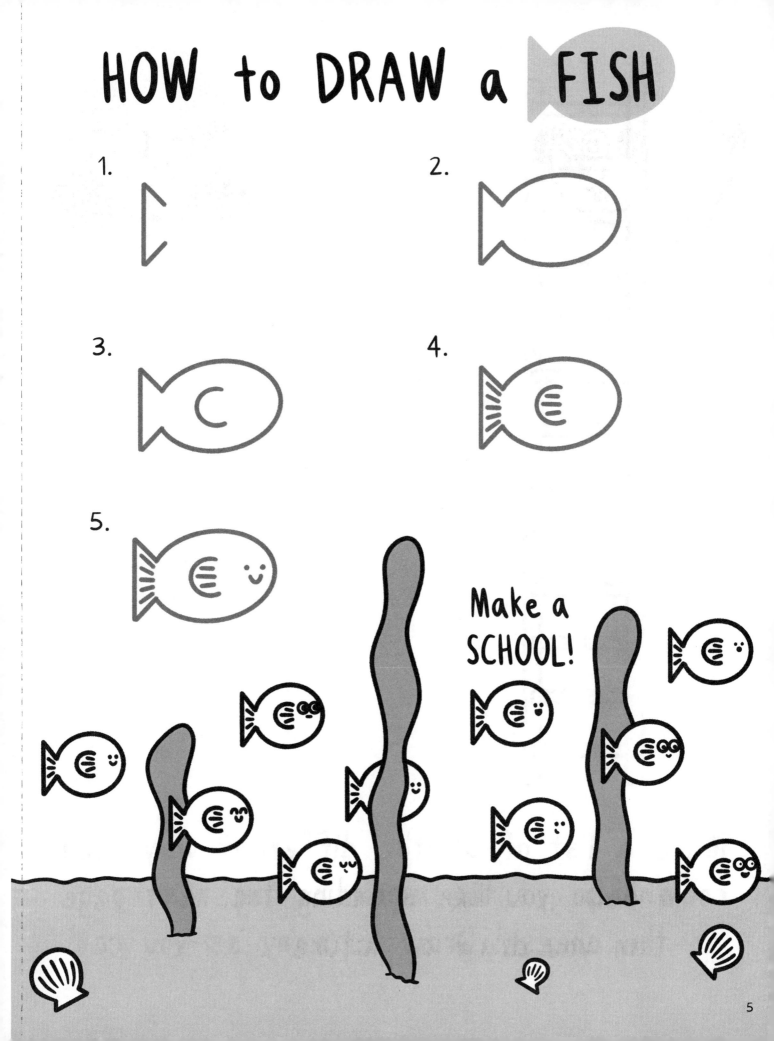

1.

2.

3.

4.

5.

Make a SCHOOL!

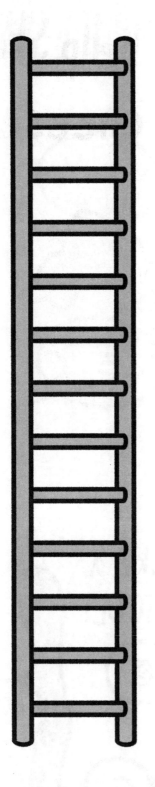

Make a list of all the different ways you could help get the mouse on the next page to the cheese! Draw as many as you can!

Draw something to help this mouse reach the cheese!

Do you have a favorite article of clothing?
Why is it your favorite?
Can you draw a picture of it?

HOW to DRAW a B O W

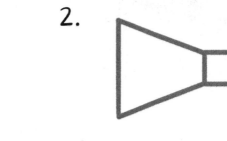

1.

2.

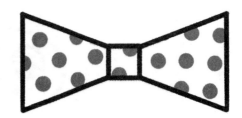

3.

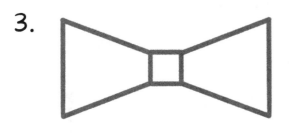

Decorate it!

Dress up your drawings!

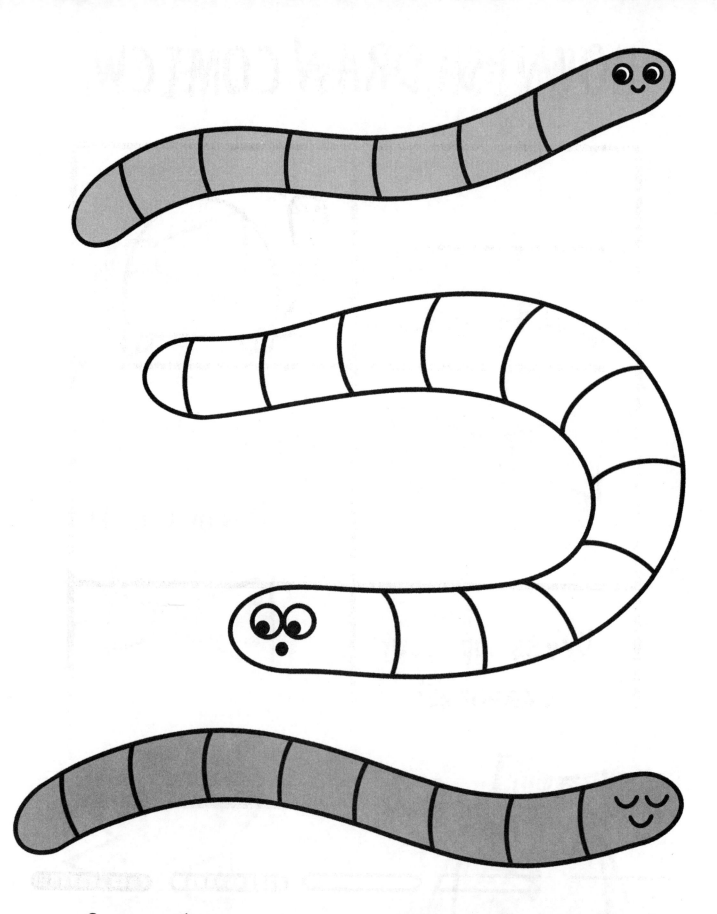

Give these worms some cool tattoos!

FINISH this COMIC!

HELLO
MY NAME IS

Is there a story behind how you were named? Does your name have a particular meaning? What does it mean to you?

Name each of these cacti!

Can you write or draw a story about
one, some, or all of them?

Write about a time that you felt left out, left behind, or lost....

FINISH this COMIC!

Write about a day you are looking forward to! Is there a day later this week? Next month? In a year?

Where is everyone hurrying?

Write or draw a story about what they will do once they get there!

Do you like bugs? Why or why not?
What other kinds of bugs can you draw?
Can you make up any of your very own?

HOW to DRAW a SPIDERWEB

1.

2.

3.

4.

5.

6.

7.

What do you think this cat is feeling?
Have you ever felt like the cat?
What made you feel better?

FINISH this COMIC!

Make a map of a room in your house,
or of your whole neighborhood!
What landmarks will you include? Why?

Decide what the symbols on this map mean!

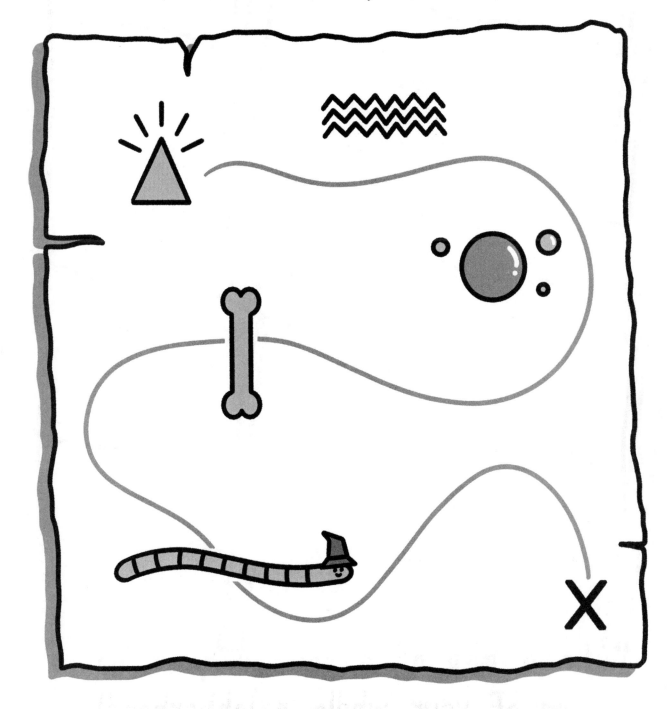

Who made the map? Why?

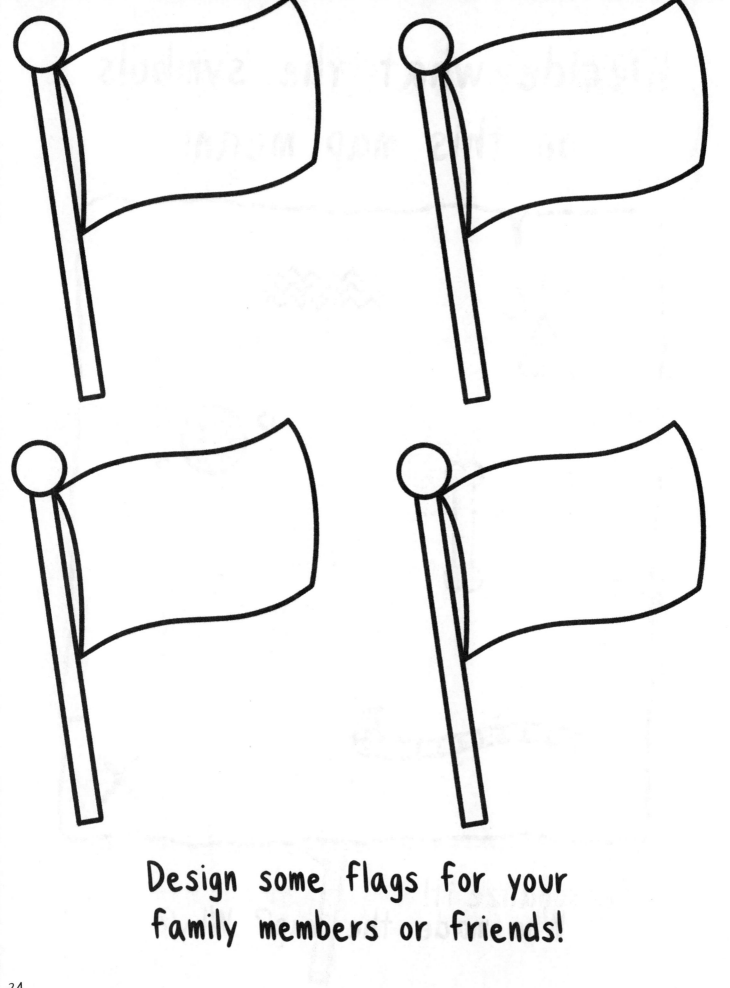

Design some flags for your
family members or friends!

HOW to DRAW a FLAG

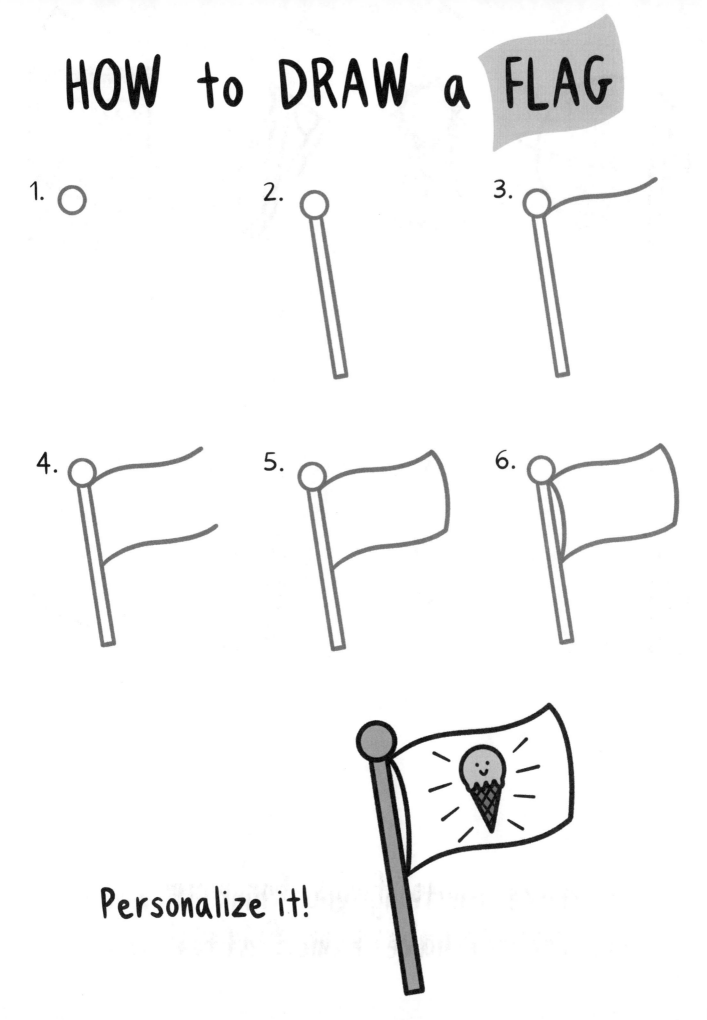

1.

2.

3.

4.

5.

6.

Personalize it!

Is there anything you think it would
be cool to have named after you?

Create a _____ sandwich!

Your name here!

Draw your ingredients between the slices of bread!

How much would your sandwich cost if it were sold in a restaurant?

Write about the time in your life that
you laughed the hardest!
Can you explain what was so funny?

FINISH this COMIC!

Hee hee...

HAHAHAHAHAHAHA HAHAHAHAHAHAHA!

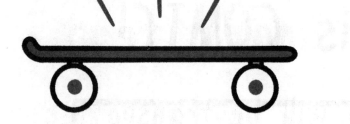

Do you have a favorite way to get around? Why is it your favorite?

This is no ordinary tent!

Step inside, and you will be transported wherever you want to go!

Where would you use the tent to go?
What would you do there?

Have you ever unexpectedly found
something AWESOME?

FINISH this COMIC!

Do you like hot or cold
weather better? Why?

HOW to DRAW a CACTUS

1.

2.

3.

4.

5.

Make it
ENORMOUS!

What are your hopes for the future?
What do you want to be different?
What would you like to be the same?

WHOA!

This kid has traveled back in time to give you a super important message!

What is the message?
Write or draw a story about what
you would do after you heard it!

Do you have a special skill
or unique talent?

HOW to DRAW a WHALE

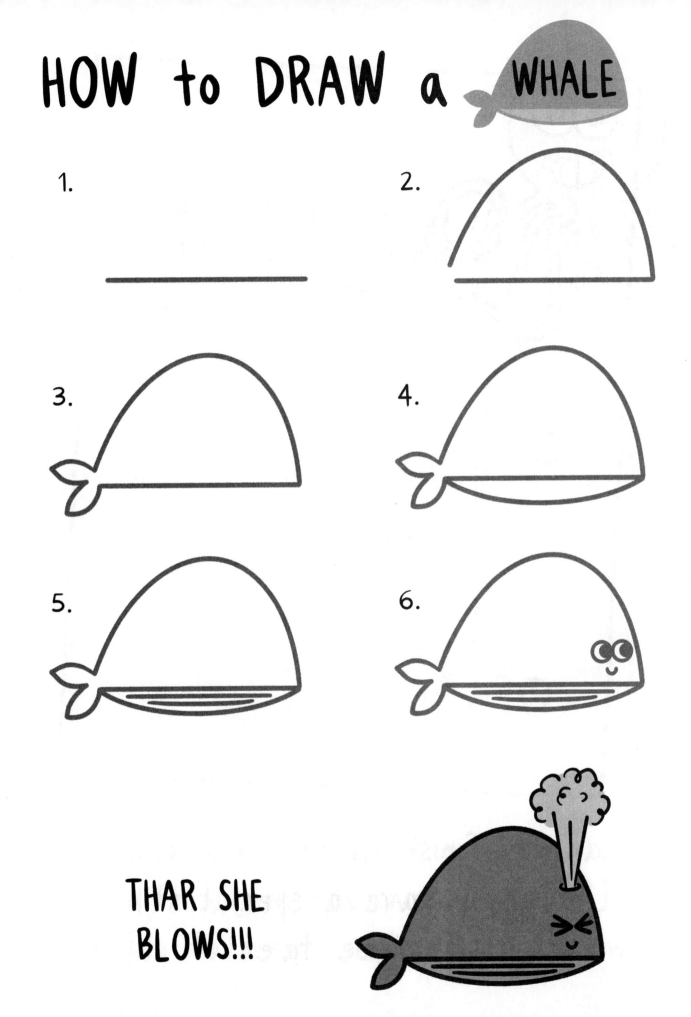

1.

2.

3.

4.

5.

6.

THAR SHE
BLOWS!!!

It was the scent that woke me up. I had never smelled anything like it. It was...

Can you finish writing this story? If you run out of room, continue writing on another sheet of paper!

FINISH this COMIC!

YOUR PICTURE HERE!

WORLD RECORD HOLDER!

Are there any records you would like to see someone break? Are there any records you think YOU could break?

This duck is a WORLD RECORD HOLDER!

Decide what record the duck broke! Write or draw a story about the duck breaking it!

Draw some hats on these characters' heads!

Draw some hats on these characters' heads!

FINISH this COMIC!

YOUR PICTURE HERE!

Are there any records you would like to see someone break? Are there any records you think YOU could break?

This duck is a WORLD RECORD HOLDER

WORLD RECORD HOLDER

Decide what record the duck bro
Write or draw a story about the
breaking it!

FINISH this COMIC!

Can you come up with a story involving
the three things above?

HOW to DRAW a VOLCANO

1.

2.

3.

4.

5.

Make it ERUPT!

Draw something falling out of the sky,
and come up with a reason why
the kid above is so happy about it.

FINISH this COMIC!

Design your own dream house!
Make a list of all the things it would
have in it, then draw a picture of it!

HOW to DRAW a CASTLE

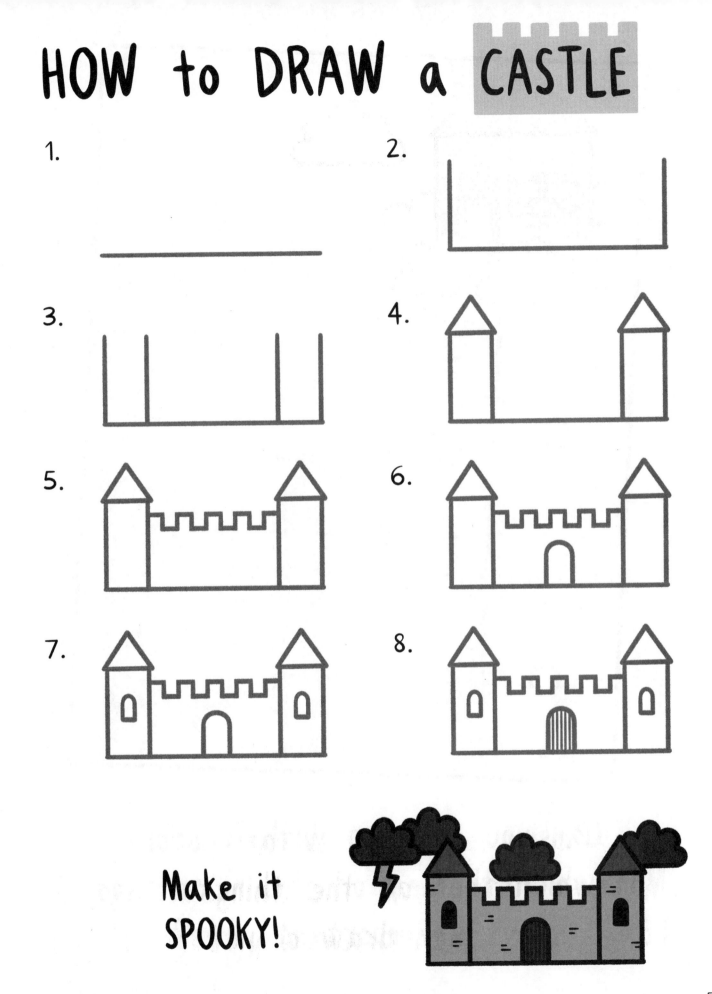

1.

2.

3.

4.

5.

6.

7.

8.

Make it SPOOKY!

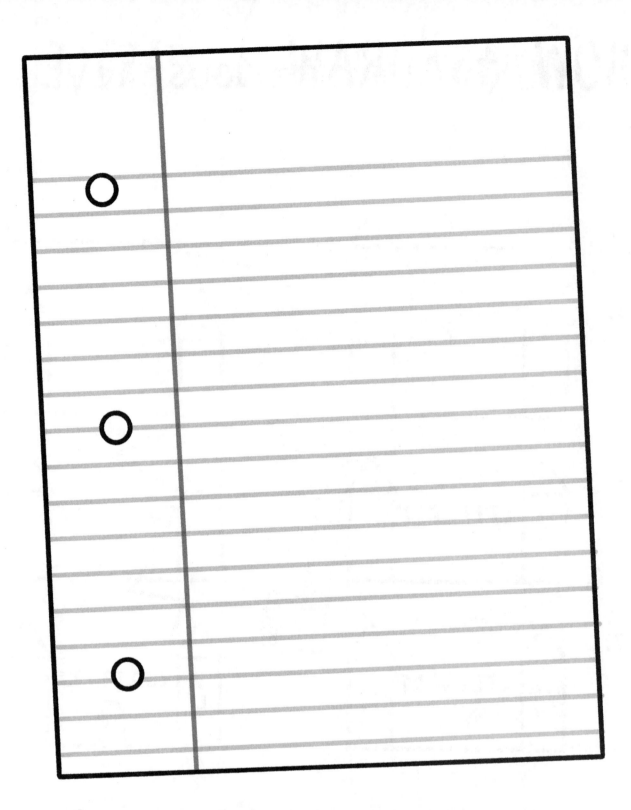

Can you come up with a story
in which the key on the next page
plays an important part?

LOOK! A mysterious key!

Decide what the key opens, then draw a picture of what's inside!

Have you ever accidentally broken
or ruined something?

FINISH this COMIC!

Can you think of any other kinds of hats?
How many of them can you draw?
Can you make up your own kind of hat?

HOW to DRAW HATS

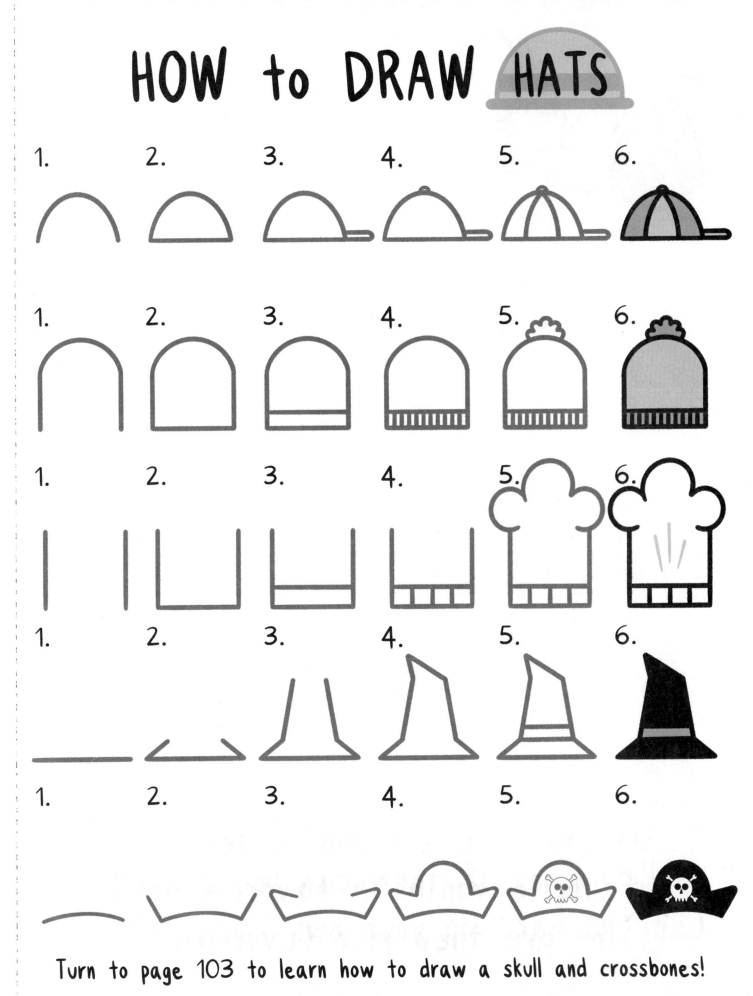

1. 2. 3. 4. 5. 6.

1. 2. 3. 4. 5. 6.

1. 2. 3. 4. 5. 6.

1. 2. 3. 4. 5. 6.

1. 2. 3. 4. 5. 6.

Turn to page 103 to learn how to draw a skull and crossbones!

Do you have a favorite season?
A favorite month? A favorite day?
Why are they your favorites?

Create a schedule for the BEST DAY EVER!

9 a.m.	
10 a.m.	
11 a.m.	
12 p.m.	
1 p.m.	
2 p.m.	
3 p.m.	
4 p.m.	
5 p.m.	
6 p.m.	
7 p.m.	
8 p.m.	
9 p.m.	
10 p.m.	

Decide what you want to do, who you want to be with, where you want to go, and what you want to eat!

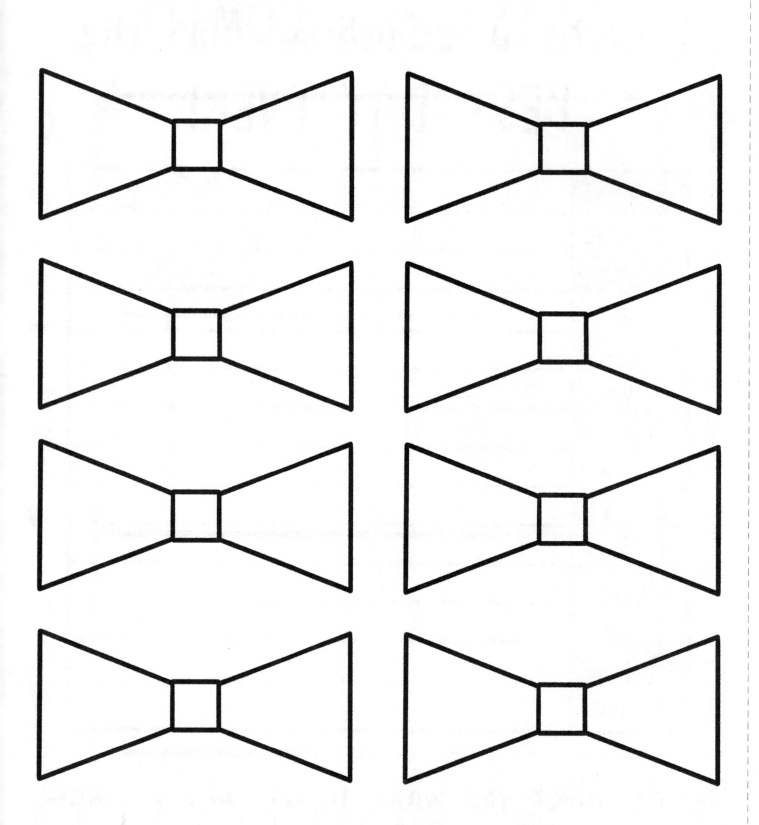

Design some special bows for some family members or friends!

FINISH this COMIC!

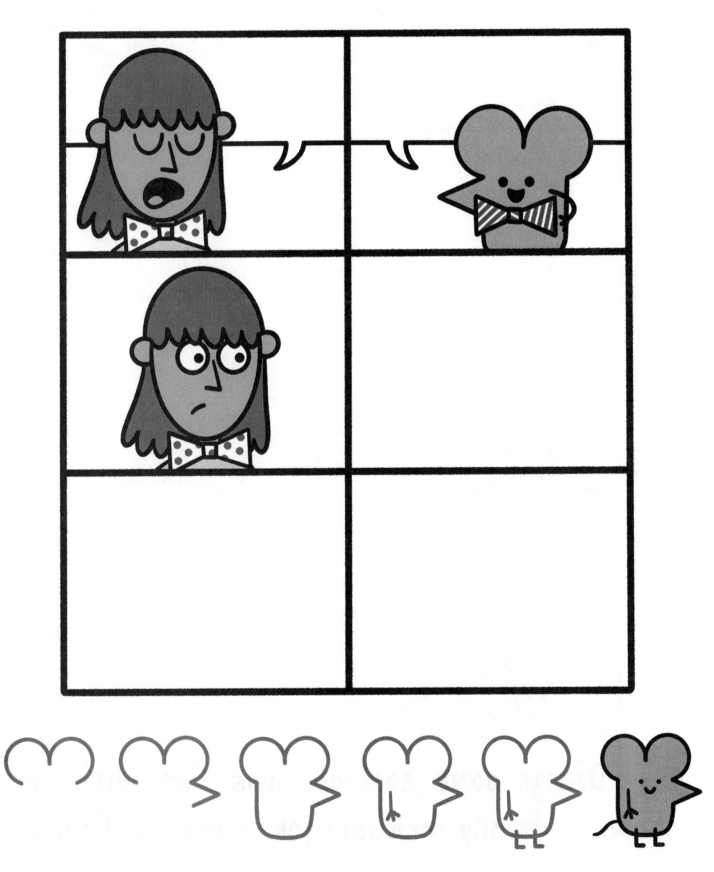

How many ways can you come up with to show that someone or something is flying?

HOW to DRAW a "BAT"

1.

2.

3.

4.

5.

6.

7.

8.

Make
it FLY!

Write about a time you played a joke on someone or someone played a joke on you!

FINISH this COMIC!

Give each of the creatures on the
next page a name! Can you imagine
a story featuring one or more of them?

Why are these sea creatures so disappointed?

Can you draw anything to cheer them up?

Is there any animal or insect that you wish you could talk with? What would you talk about?

FINISH this COMIC!

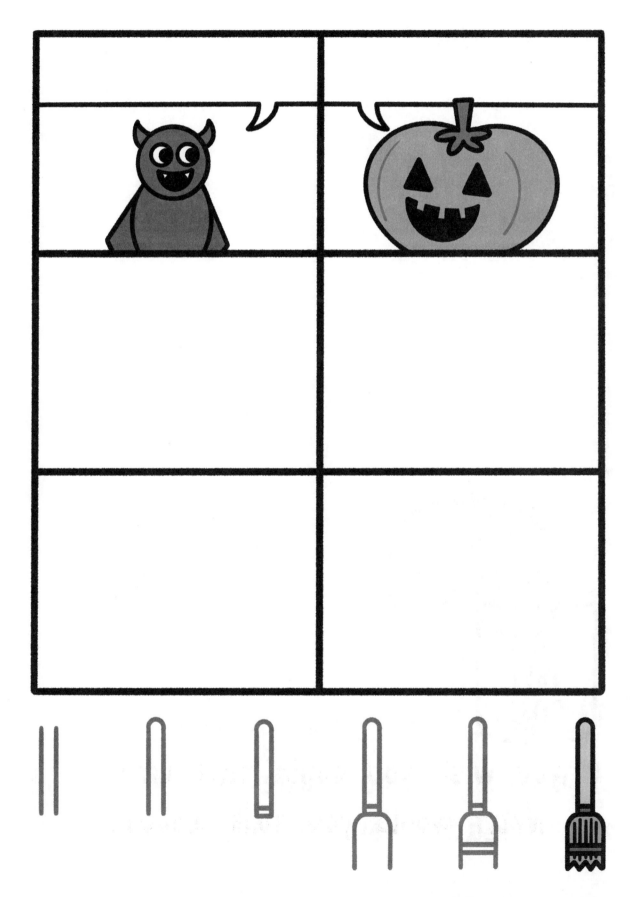

What makes a good leader? Have you ever had to lead? Would you ever want to?

HOW to DRAW a CROWN

1.

2.

3.

4.

5.

6.

Make it SPARKLE!

If you could instantly change something about the world, what would it be? Why?

FINISH this COMIC!

Can you think of any other words for the emotions on the next page? How many other feelings can you name? Try to draw them!

Name the emotions each of these kids is showing!

What puts you in each of these moods?
What makes you change from one to another?

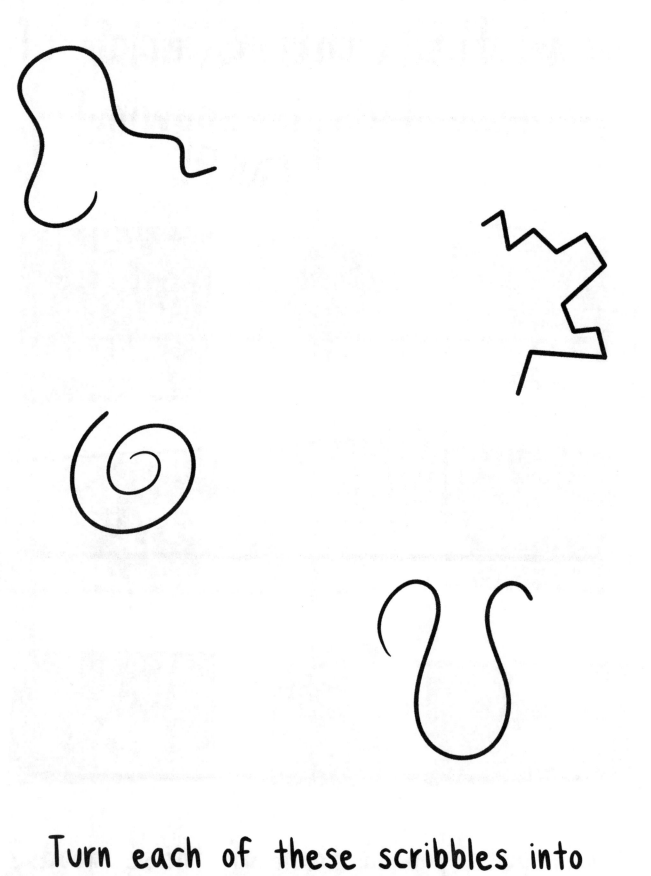

Turn each of these scribbles into
a finished drawing!

FINISH this COMIC!

1.

2.

3.

4.

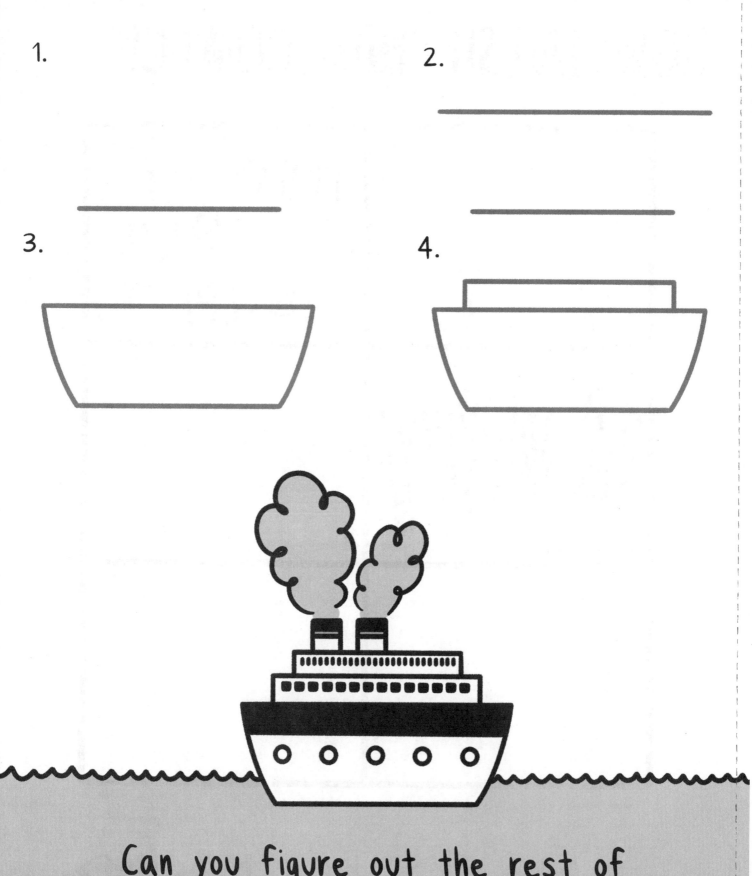

Can you figure out the rest of the steps to draw a BIG boat?

HOW to DRAW a LIGHTHOUSE

1.

2.

3.

4.

5.

6.

7.

8.

Make it SHINE!

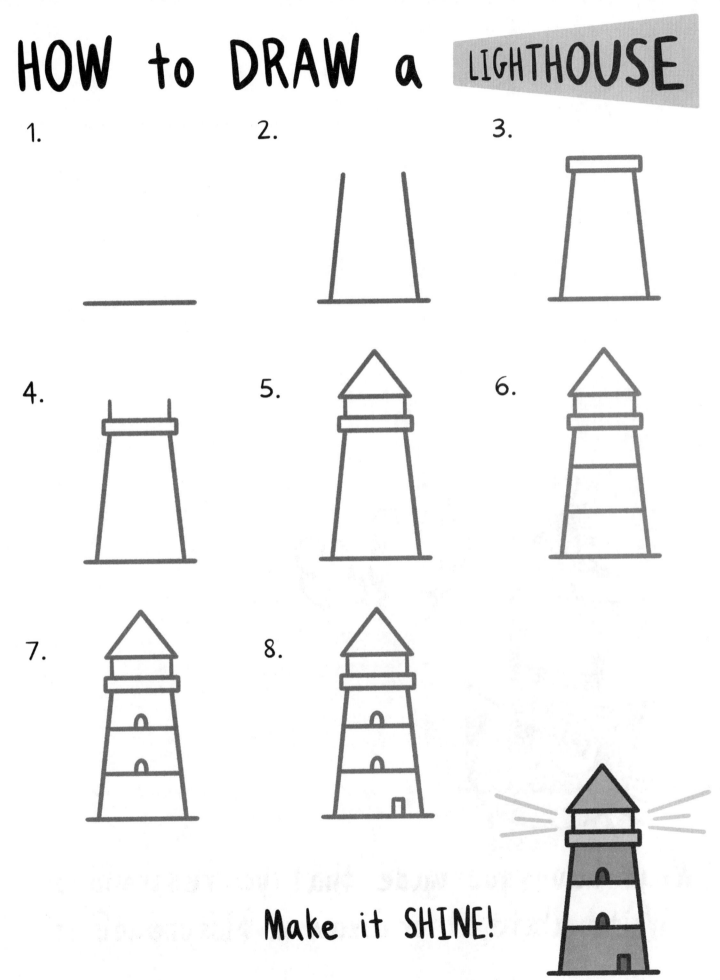

What have you made that you're proud of?
Write about it or draw a picture of it!

FINISH this COMIC!

Have you ever had to do something scary?

Where do you think this path leads?

Write or draw a story about someone who has to go down it!

Design and decorate these pumpkins!

HOW to DRAW a

1.

2.

3.

4.

5.

Decide what's in these jars, then make
some labels for them!

FINISH this COMIC!

Is there anything that you used to be
afraid of that you're not afraid of now?
Is there any fear that you hope
to conquer one day?

HOW to DRAW a PLANE

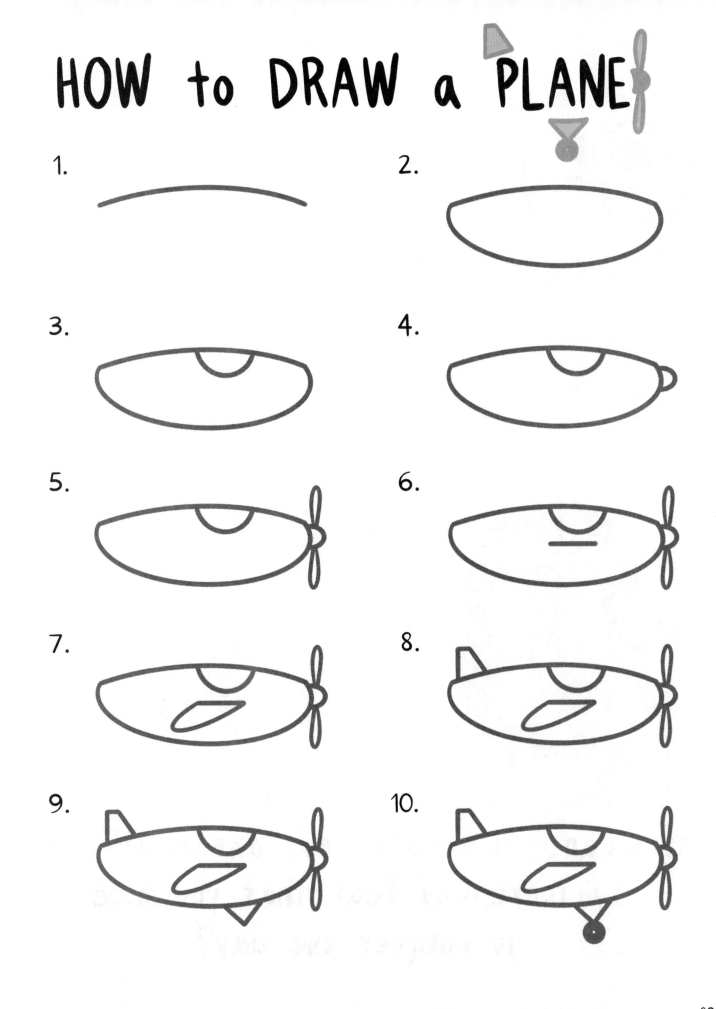

1.

2.

3.

4.

5.

6.

7.

8.

9.

10.

Can you create your own code?
Can you think of any times it would be
useful to have one?

Use this code to write a secret note!

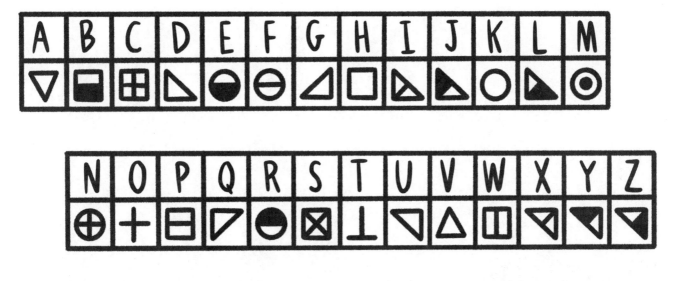

A = ▽, B = ▣, C = ⊞, D = ◿, etc.

Has a wish of yours ever come true?

WOW! A wish fish!

Whatever you wish for will come true!
What will it be?

Write about a time you felt embarrassed.
Why did you feel that way?
Do you feel any different
about the experience now?

FINISH this COMIC!

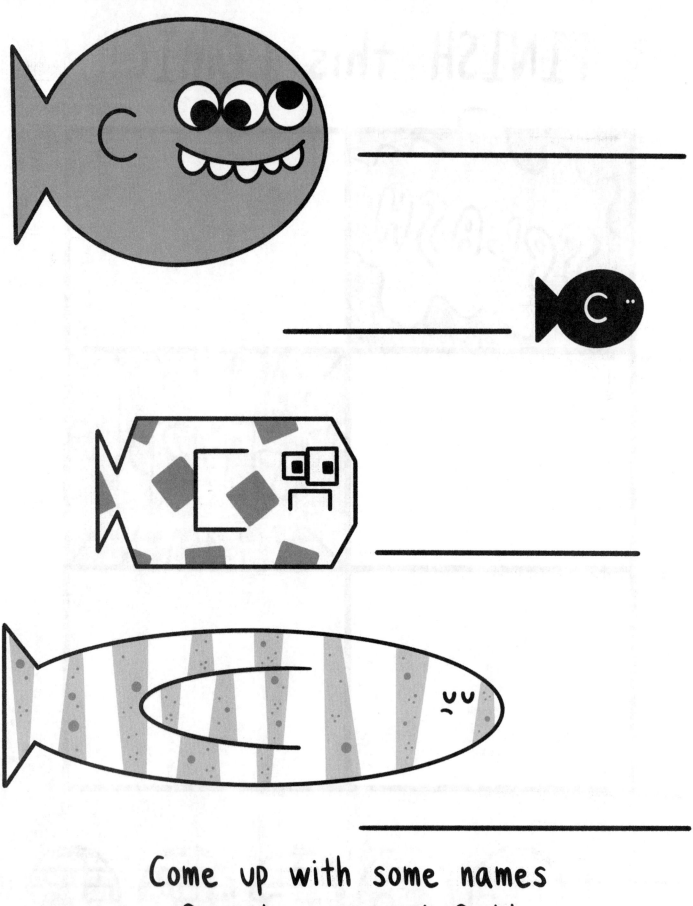

Come up with some names
for these weird fish!

HOW to DRAW a BLOWFISH

1.

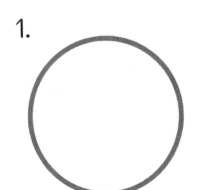

2.

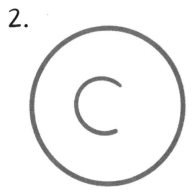

3.

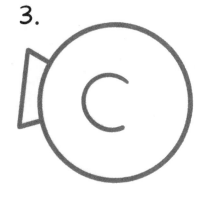

4.

5.

6.

7.

8.

What do you do to relax?
Is there anywhere in particular
that you like to relax?

QUICK! Draw something to cool off this volcano!

What do you think your food would say
if it could talk to you?

FINISH this COMIC!

Can you figure out how to draw
the rest of this skeleton?

HOW to DRAW a SKULL and CROSSBONES

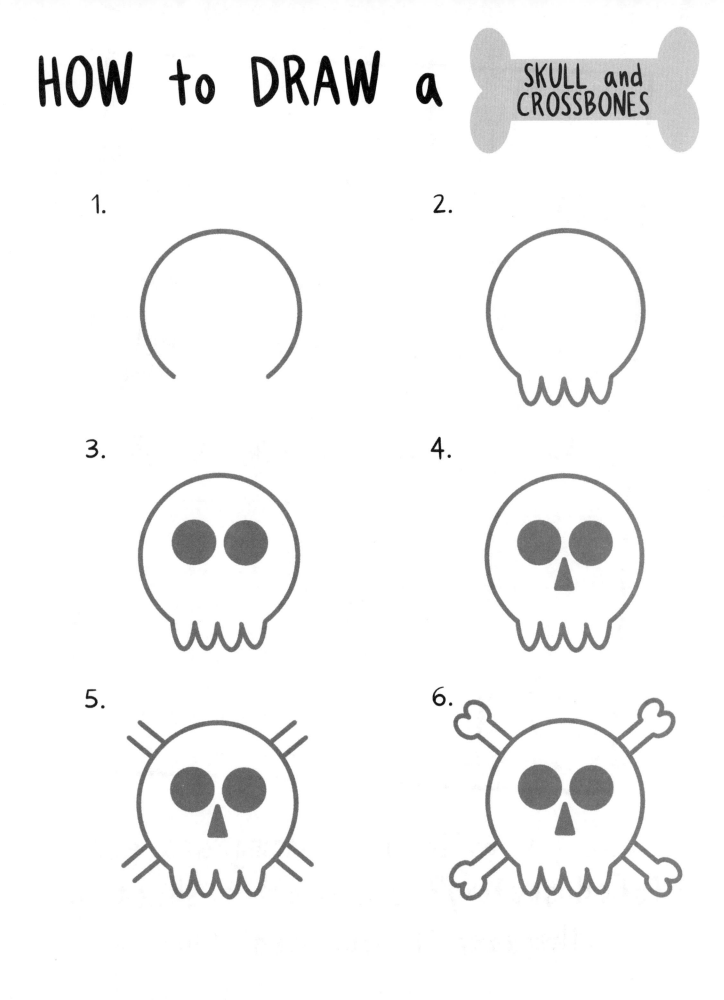

1.

2.

3.

4.

5.

6.

All of a sudden, my best friend came crashing out of the building.

"RUN!" she cried. "RUN FOR YOUR LIFE!"

Can you write a beginning and end for this story? Use another sheet of paper if you need to!

FINISH this COMIC!

How many different ways can you
come up with to draw eyes?

Use dots and lines to make eyes, mouths, and eyebrows for these mice!

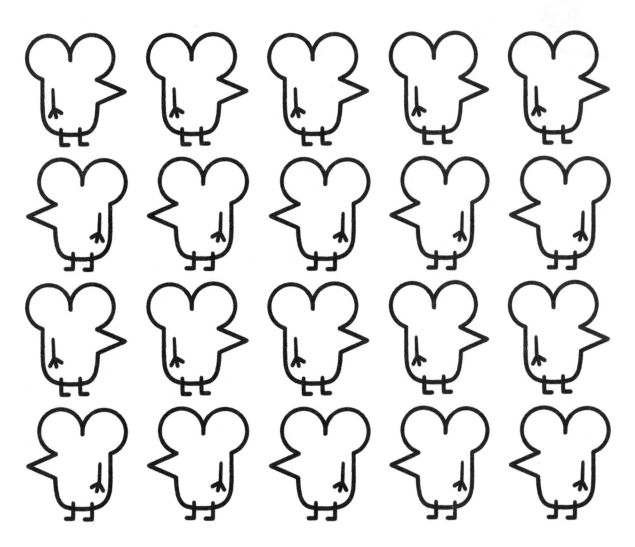

How many different expressions can you draw? Are any emotions harder to show than others?

Create some keys of your own! Don't forget to decide what each of them opens!

HOW to DRAW KEYS

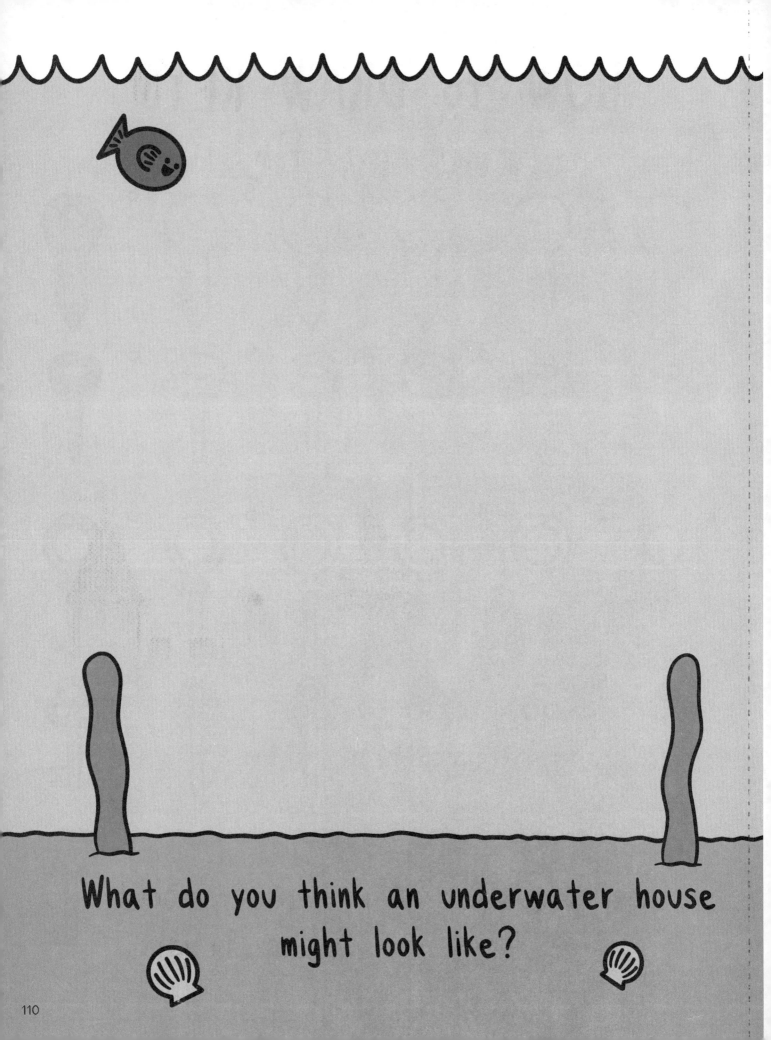

What do you think an underwater house
might look like?

Decide who lives in this castle!

Now write or draw a story about something that happens in it!

Have you ever broken a bone or gotten injured? Write about how it happened and what it was like!

FINISH this COMIC!

How many different kinds of plants can you name? How many of them can you draw?

FINISH this COMIC!

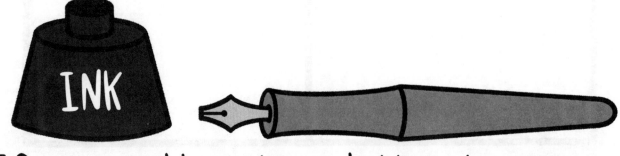

If you could write a letter to someone
from the past, who would it be?
What would you say to them?

What messages are these planes flying?

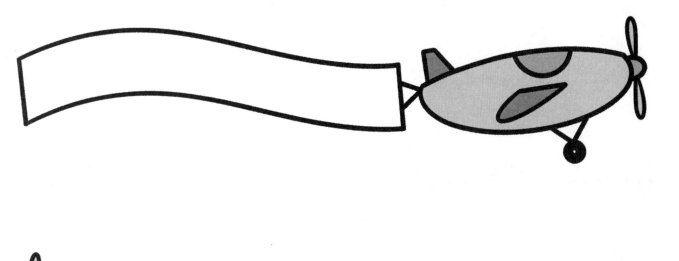

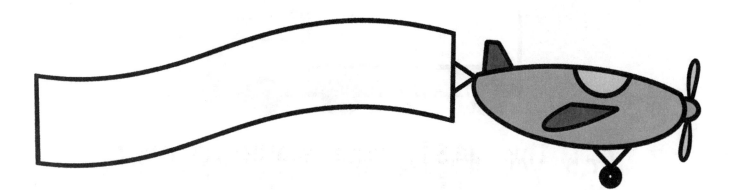

1.

2.

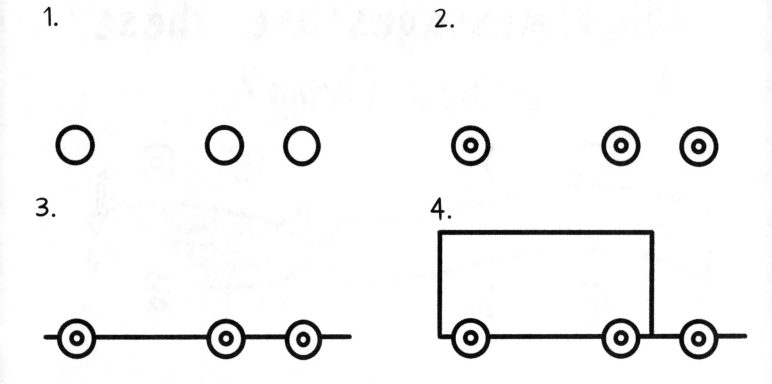

3.

4.

Can you figure out the rest of the steps to draw a truck?

HOW to DRAW a CAR

1.

2.

3.

4.

5.

6.

7.

8.

9.

10.

Make it
MOVE!

What is something you are SUPER at doing? Is there anything you want to get better at doing?

Finish drawing this
SUPERHERO!

And don't forget to give them a name,
some powers, and a backstory!

Can you draw an overhead view of the objects above? What else can you draw an overhead view of?

HOW to DRAW a HELICOPTER

1.

2.

3.

4.

5.

6.

7.

8.

9.

10.

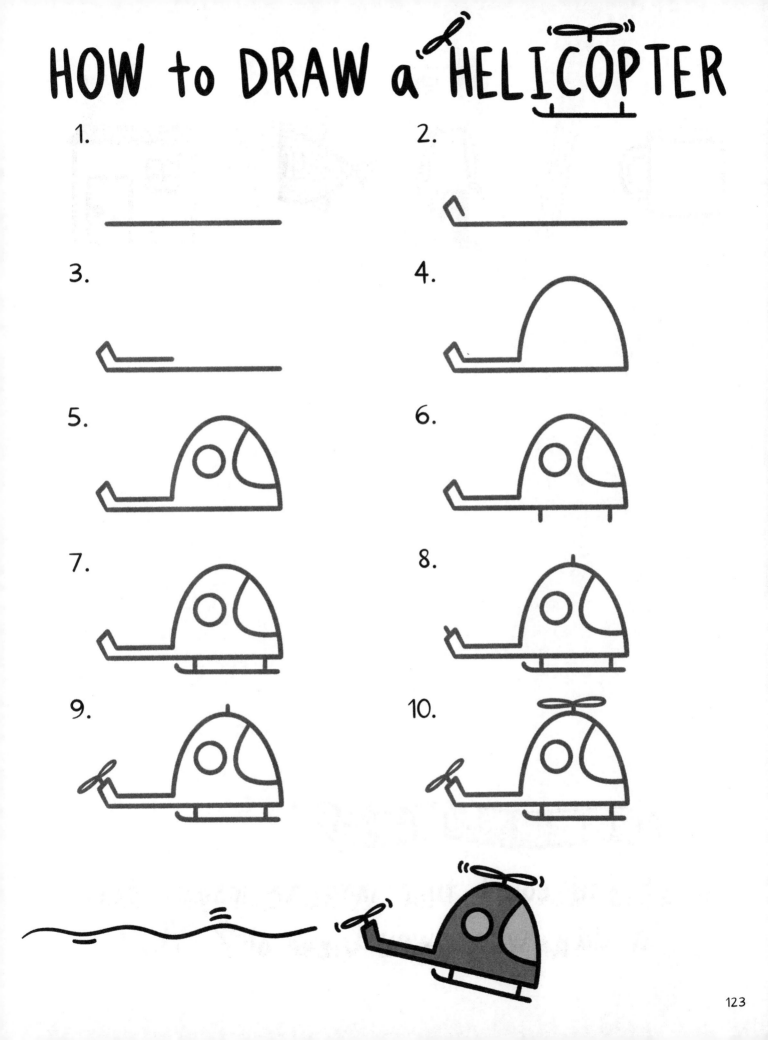

If you could turn into an insect for a day, what would you do? Why?

FINISH this COMIC!

Make up some of your own sound effects!
Can you come up with some fun
ways of lettering them?

FINISH this COMIC!

Is there anything that you used to like that you don't like now? Is there anything you don't like now that you can imagine liking in the future?

Make a self-portrait using stuff you love!

If you had a treasure chest,
what would you put in it?

HOW to DRAW a TREASURE CHEST

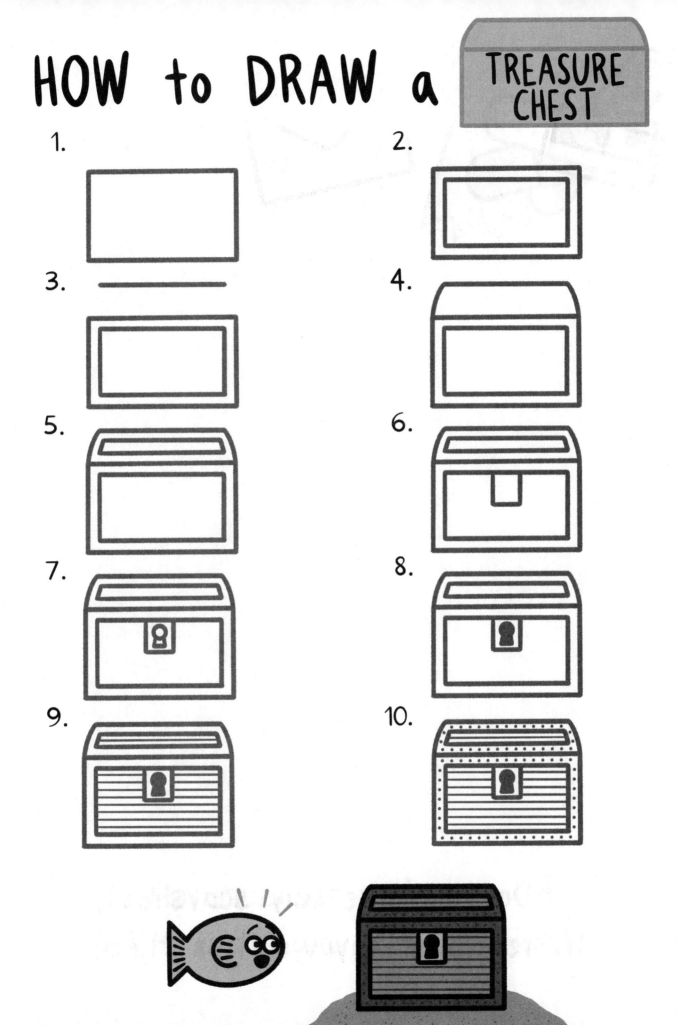

1.

2.

3.

4.

5.

6.

7.

8.

9.

10.

Do you have any scars?
Write about how you got them!

Check out this pirate's scARRRs!

Write or draw a story about how they got them all!

Do you have a favorite cold-weather activity? Why is it your favorite?

HOW to DRAW SNOWFLAKES

1.   2.   3.   4.   5.   6.

1.   2.   3.   4.   5.   6.

1.   2.   3.   4.   5.   6.

1.   2.   3.   4.   5.   6.

Is there anywhere you want to travel to?
What would you like to do there?

FINISH this COMIC!

HOW to DRAW

1.

2.

3.

4.

5.

6.

7.

8.

9.

Make your own How to Draw instructions!
Try them out on a family member or friend!

Make Your Own COMIC!

BONUS ACTIVITIES

If you've finished all the activities in this book, and you still want more, there are a few things you can do.

You can:

· check out my other activity book, GIVE THIS BOOK A TITLE.

· redo some of the activities, trying something different than you originally did.

· visit my website, www.jarrettlerner.com, and go to the ACTIVITIES page, where you'll find a lot more activities like those in this book, all of them available to download and print for free.

· combine two or more of the activities in this book to create your own brand-new prompt. Below, I've shared some examples of how you might do this. But the possibilities are literally endless!

1. Imagine the sloth on page 68 met the wish fish on page 93. What do you think the sloth would wish for? Why?

2. Imagine if the pirate on page 133 was designing a dream house, like you did on page 50. What things would the house have in it? Can you draw a picture of the house?

3. Imagine the cat in the crown on page 73 was making a self-portrait of stuff they loved, like you did on page 129. What would the cat's self-portrait look like?

I hope this book has helped you become a more confident and capable creator than you were when you first opened it.

I hope you continue to explore and express your creativity, and that you'll share it with the world.

Remember:

THERE IS NO RIGHT OR WRONG WAY TO CREATE.

And while you're creating, don't be afraid to mess up, to make mistakes. I make mistakes every day while writing and drawing—a LOT of them. But every mistake is an opportunity to learn. To get a little better.

Last, but definitely not least:

HaVE fUn!

JARRett!!